Food from the G

by Elsie and Denis W
pictures by Denis Wrigley

Published by Dinosaur Publications

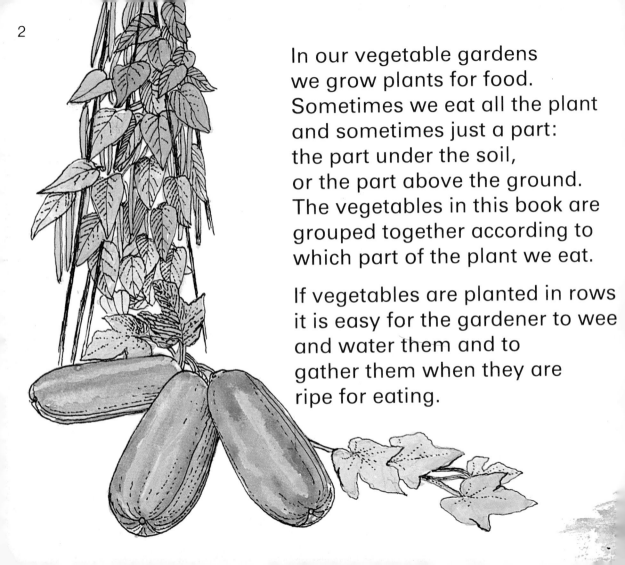

In our vegetable gardens
we grow plants for food.
Sometimes we eat all the plant
and sometimes just a part:
the part under the soil,
or the part above the ground.
The vegetables in this book are
grouped together according to
which part of the plant we eat.

If vegetables are planted in rows
it is easy for the gardener to wee
and water them and to
gather them when they are
ripe for eating.

Food under the ground — tubers

Potatoes are tubers, and grow along the roots of the plant. They are planted in rows and covered with a mound of soil. Small potatoes or cut pieces, each with an 'eye', are used. When the white flowers come out it is time to dig up the the plants. Underneath are lots of fresh new potatoes. Some will be quite small. If bigger ones are wanted they are left until later in the year.

Potatoes

Old potatoes are then dug up and put into sacks to store for the winter. Sometimes they are stacked all together outside and a big heap of soil piled on top – this is called a *clamp*.

A sack of Potatoes

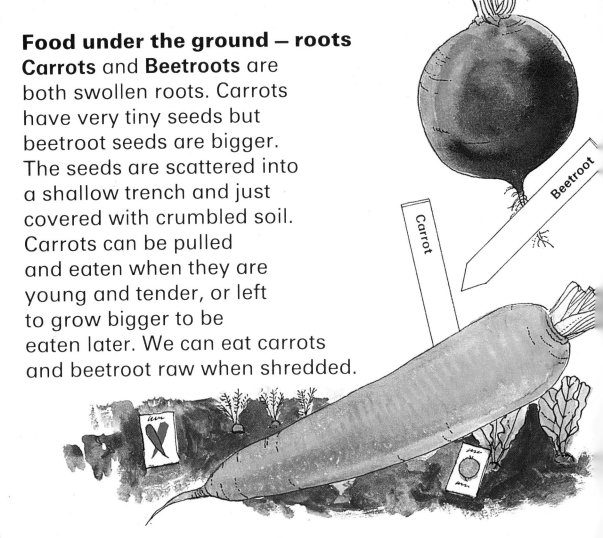

Food under the ground — roots

Carrots and **Beetroots** are both swollen roots. Carrots have very tiny seeds but beetroot seeds are bigger. The seeds are scattered into a shallow trench and just covered with crumbled soil. Carrots can be pulled and eaten when they are young and tender, or left to grow bigger to be eaten later. We can eat carrots and beetroot raw when shredded.

Beetroot

Carrot

We eat the swollen roots of **radishes** raw in salads. They grow very quickly and can be sown between other rows of vegetables.

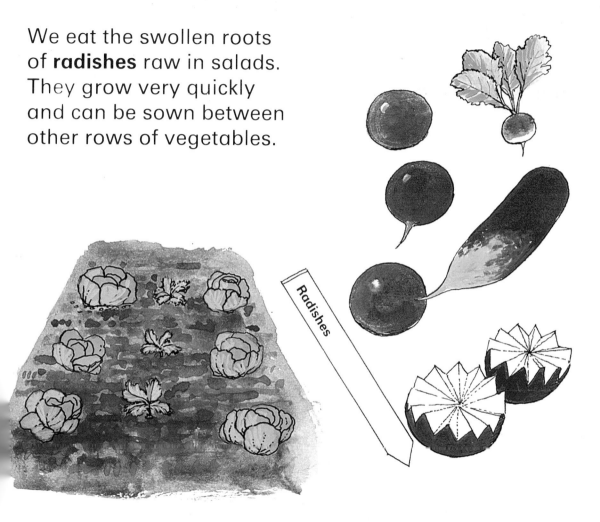

Radishes

Turnips are best eaten when they are young. The gardener brushes away the soil from each plant before pulling it to make sure there is a nice round root.

Parsnips grow into big plants, and they need a lot of space between them. They will keep in the soil in winter.

Turnip

Parsnip

You can make a lantern from a big **swede** to hang outside in the autumn. Scoop out all the centre to cook as a nice golden vegetable. Cut a face in the skin and put a lighted candle inside.

Swedes

Stems and bulbs to eat

To make the long swollen
stems of **leeks** white
they have a paper collar
around them as they grow.

Onions can be dried in the sun
and stored hanging
on a string or in an
old stocking.

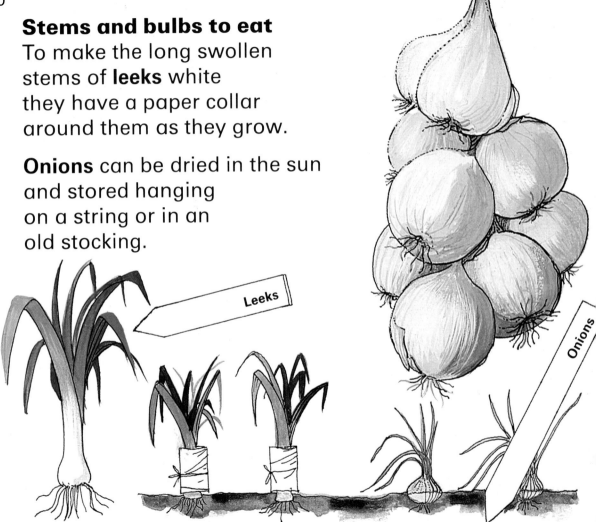

Leeks

Onions

Stems to eat

Asparagus is grown under mounds of earth. When the tips reach to the top of the soil the long white stems are cut out of the mound. Some kinds of **celery** have pale stems; others need to wear a collar to keep them white and tender.

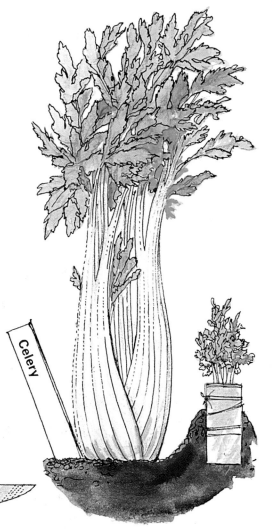

Asparagus

Celery

12

Buds to eat

Sprouts grow a rosette of
leaves at the top of the
plant which we can eat.
But we mainly grow the plant
for the tight little buds
that grow up the stem. They
are cut off to be cooked
when we want to eat them.

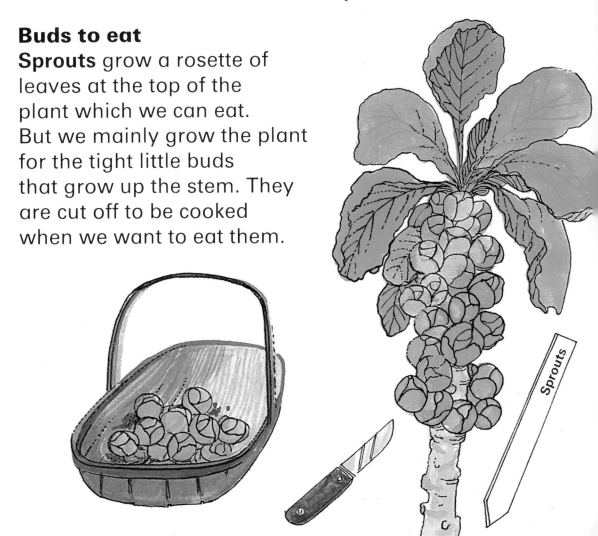

Leaves to eat

There are many varieties of **cabbage**. Some are grown to be eaten at different times of the year. Winter cabbages are round and hard and heavy and they can be hung up in a dry place to store. Spring cabbages have much darker, looser green leaves.

Winter Cabbage

Spring Cabbage

Leaves to eat

If a few seeds are sown
every two weeks throughout
the spring and summer,
lettuces will grow in the
garden from spring to autumn.
There are many kinds.
Plants covered with glass
or plastic keep warm, and
grow more quickly in the spring.

Cos Lettuce

Cabbage Lettuce

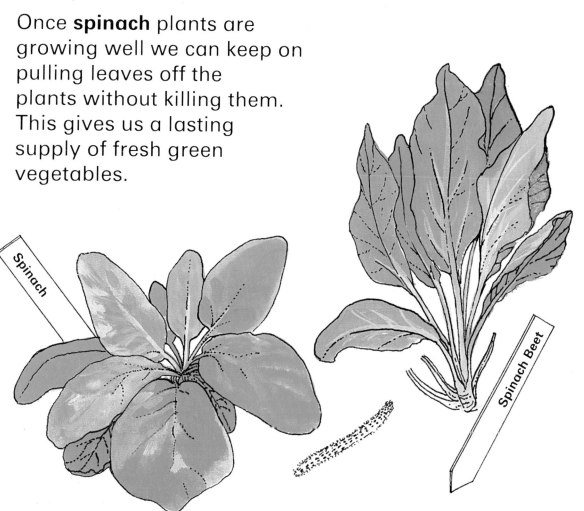

Once **spinach** plants are growing well we can keep on pulling leaves off the plants without killing them. This gives us a lasting supply of fresh green vegetables.

Spinach

Spinach Beet

Flowers to eat

We eat the tight white
flower buds from the
centre of the **cauliflower**
plant. They form
a close, solid white
head.

Cauliflower

Sprouting broccoli
makes spear-shaped stems
of buds, either purple
or green. These must be
eaten whilst the buds
are tight. It is too late
to pick them for eating when
the buds have opened into
flowers.

Sprouting Broccoli

Vegetable fruits to eat

We usually scoop the seeds out of the **marrow** before we cook it. Sometimes we stuff the space that is left with savoury things. **Courgettes** (tiny marrows) are eaten small, skin, seeds and all.

Courgettes

Marrow

Cucumbers and **tomatoes** are usually eaten in salads. They taste specially good raw when very fresh but they are good cooked too. Some cucumbers can be grown in the open, some need protection under glass.

Tomatoes

Cucumbers

Seeds to eat

Sweetcorn depends on
the wind to pollinate
the seeds. To be sure of
a good crop, the seeds are
planted in a block together.
When the seeds are just
turning golden it can be
cooked as a vegetable.
It is also harvested as
grain (much later) when
the seeds are ripe and dry
and sometimes used to make
cornflakes and cooking oil.

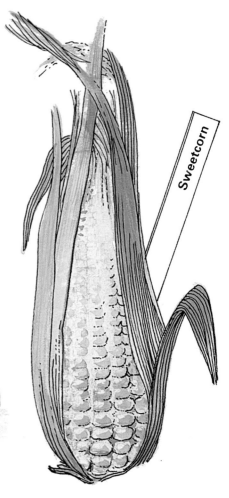

Sweetcorn

Some **beans** grow in thick fluffy pods to protect the seeds which we eat. Others have round or flat pods and when the seeds are tiny we can eat the pods whole. Other beans are left to ripen and when dried they can be stored. These beans usually have to be soaked before they can be cooked.

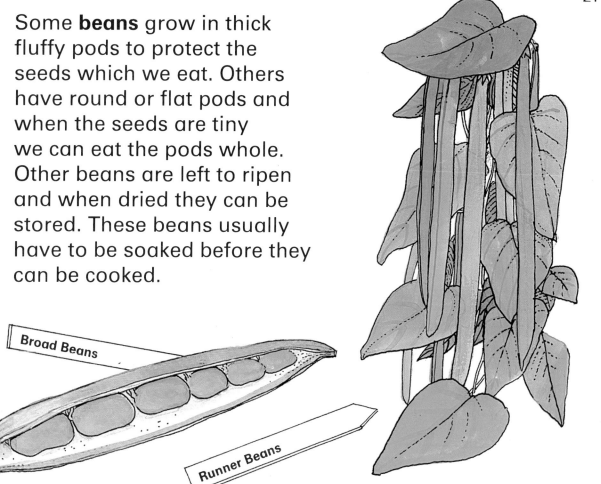

Broad Beans

Runner Beans

Seeds to eat

Peas are seeds and,
as well as eating them,
we save some to plant. These
will grow into next year's
pea plants. The small dry
peas are planted in rows.
Sticks are put in to protect
the young plants as they
grow. The plants put out
tendrils to hold on to the
sticks. After a few weeks
flower buds grow and open.
Insects crawl in, collect
pollen and scatter it in
other flowers.

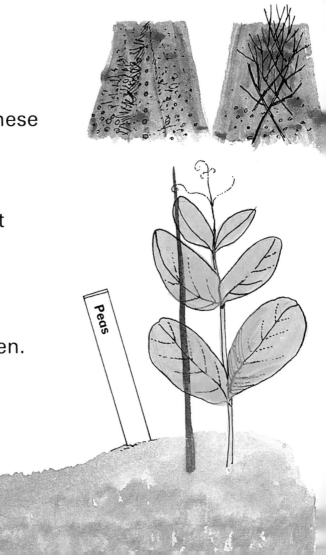

Peas

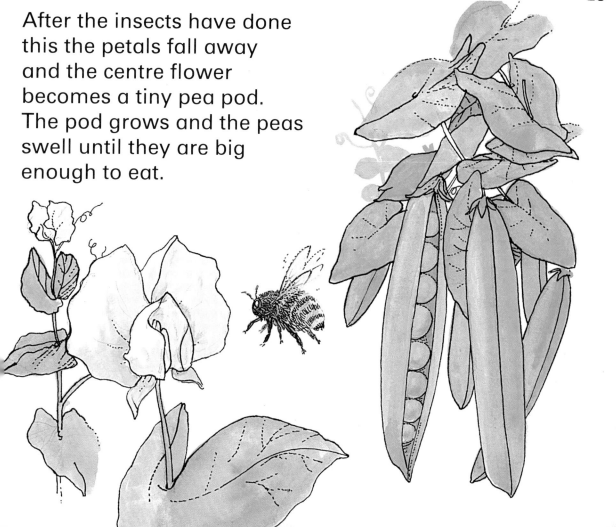

After the insects have done
this the petals fall away
and the centre flower
becomes a tiny pea pod.
The pod grows and the peas
swell until they are big
enough to eat.

Here are some other vegetables that grow easily. Find out which name goes with which plant.

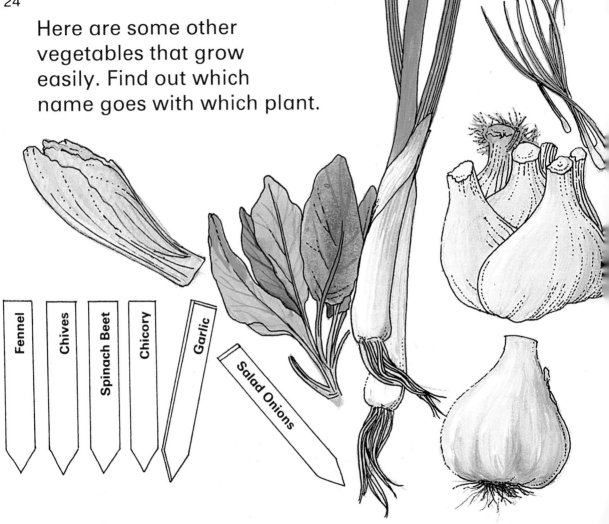

Fennel

Chives

Spinach Beet

Chicory

Garlic

Salad Onions